LIFE CHANGING GRATITUDE

YOUR SHORTCUT TO AUTHENTIC HAPPINESS

A collection of gratitude quotes and accompanying color nature photographs

BY
MATT BLOHOWIAK

FIRST PUBLISHED 2016
© 2016 MATT BLOHOWIAK

EDITORS: Sarah Pederson, Gail Blohowiak
PHOTOGRAPHS: Pixabay, Michelle Buntin, Matt Blohowiak, Sarah Pederson

All rights reserved, including the right to reproduce this book or portions thereof in any form whatsoever, without the prior permission in writing of the publisher.

ISBN-13: 978-0-9973158-1-3

Practicing gratitude throughout your day is one sure way to invite happiness into your life. Gratitude turns the ordinary into the extraordinary, inadequacy into abundance, poverty into richness, fear into love, the mundane into beauty, and entitlement into privilege.

Commit to practicing gratitude daily. You can sing it, mumble it, dance it, write it, meditate on it, or feel it with your heart. Don't worry about the negative thoughts that will enter your mind. You are human and you will stumble, but do not quit! Force gratitude on yourself, even if you don't feel it one particular day. Your good thoughts will attract more good thoughts and begin to erase the negative. Share your gift of gratitude with others and watch your life transform. You are worth it and you deserve it!

Some of the side effects of gratitude may include:

Happiness	Higher self-worth
Improved relationships	Contentment
Better sleep	Better health
Better coping skills	Spiritual connections

"Gratitude is an emotion expressing appreciation for what one has—as opposed to, for example, a consumer-driven emphasis on what one wants. Gratitude is getting a great deal of attention as a facet of positive psychology: Studies show that we can deliberately cultivate gratitude, and can increase our well-being and happiness by doing so. In addition, gratefulness—and especially expression of it to others—is associated with increased energy, optimism, and empathy."

– Psychology Today

"Cultivating an "attitude of gratitude" has been linked to better health, sounder sleep, less anxiety and depression, higher long-term satisfaction with life and kinder behavior toward others, including romantic partners."

– John Tierney, The New York Times

"Gratitude can transform common days into thanksgivings, turn routine jobs into joy and change ordinary opportunities into blessings."

– William Arthur Ward

"Gratitude is not only the greatest of virtues, but the parent of all others."

— Marcus Tullius Cicero

"This is a wonderful day. I've never seen this one before."

— Maya Angelou

"We can complain because rose bushes have thorns, or rejoice because thorn bushes have roses."

— Abraham Lincoln

"Be thankful for what you have; you'll end up having more. If you concentrate on what you don't have, you will never, ever have enough."

– Oprah Winfrey

"If a fellow isn't thankful for what he's got, he isn't likely to be thankful for what he's going to get."

—   Frank A. Clark

"We must find time to stop and thank the people who make a difference in our lives."

– John F. Kennedy

"Cultivate the habit of being grateful for every good thing that comes to you, and to give thanks continuously. And because all things have contributed to your advancement, you should include all things in your gratitude."

— Ralph Waldo Emerson

"The unthankful heart discovers no mercies; but the thankful heart will find, in every hour, some heavenly blessings."

- Henry Ward Beecher

"I still miss those I loved who are no longer with me but I find I am grateful for having loved them. The gratitude has finally conquered the loss."

— Rita Mae Brown

"Feeling grateful or appreciative of someone or something in your life actually attracts more of the things that you appreciate and value into your life."

– Christiane Northrup

"Gratitude is one of the sweet shortcuts to finding peace of mind and happiness inside. No matter what is going on outside of us, there's always something we could be grateful for."

– Barry Neil Kaufman

"In ordinary life we hardly realize that we receive a great deal more than we give, and that it is only with gratitude that life becomes rich."

– Dietrich Bonhoeffer

"I try hard to hold fast to the truth that a full and thankful heart cannot entertain great conceits. When brimming with gratitude, one's heartbeat must surely result in outgoing love, the finest emotion we can ever know."

— Bill W.

"Thank you is the best prayer that anyone could say. I say that one a lot. Thank you expresses extreme gratitude, humility, understanding."

– Alice Walker

"None is more impoverished than the one who has no gratitude. Gratitude is a currency that we can mint for ourselves, and spend without fear of bankruptcy."

– Fred De Witt Van Amburgh

"Gratitude always comes into play; research shows that people are happier if they are grateful for the positive things in their lives, rather than worrying about what might be missing."

— Dan Buettner

"The roots of all goodness lie in the soil of appreciation for goodness."

— Dalai Lama

"When I started counting my blessings, my whole life turned around."

– Willie Nelson

"If the only prayer you say in your life is thank you, that would suffice."

– Meister Eckhart

"Find the good and praise it."

— Alex Haley

"Gratitude is the sign of noble souls."

— Aesop

"When you practice gratefulness, there is a sense of respect towards others."

– Dalai Lama

"What if you gave someone a gift, and they neglected to thank you for it-would you be likely to give them another? Life is the same way. In order to attract more of the blessings that life has to offer, you must truly appreciate what you already have."

– Ralph Marston

"Happiness is itself a kind of gratitude."

- Joseph Wood Krutch

"Appreciation can change a day, even change a life. Your willingness to put it into words is all that is necessary."

— Margaret Cousins

"If you are really thankful, what do you do? You share."

- W. Clement Stone

"Look at everything as though you were seeing it for the first or the last time, then your time on earth will be filled with glory."

– Betty Smith

"When you give out acts of kindness, it's as though something inside your body responds and says, 'Yes, this is how I ought to feel.'"

— Rabbi Harold Kushner

"Not what we say about our blessings, but how we use them, is the true measure of our thanksgiving."

— W.T. Purkiser

"At times our own light goes out and is rekindled by a spark from another person. Each of us has cause to think with deep gratitude of those who have lighted the flame within us."

– Albert Schweitzer

"You say grace before meals. All right. But I say grace before the concert and the opera, and grace before the play and pantomime, and grace before I open a book, and grace before sketching, painting, swimming, fencing, boxing, walking, playing, dancing and grace before I dip the pen in the ink."

– G. K. Chesterton

"No duty is more urgent than that of returning thanks."

- Unknown

"Let us be grateful to people who make us happy; they are the charming gardeners who make our souls blossom."

—   Marcel Proust

"You simply will not be the same person two months from now after consciously giving thanks each day for the abundance that exists in your life. And you will have set in motion an ancient spiritual law: the more you have and are grateful for, the more will be given you."

— Sarah Ban Breathnach

"We can only be said to be alive in those moments when our hearts are conscious of our treasures."

– Thornton Wilder

"There are only two ways to live your life. One is as though nothing is a miracle. The other is as though everything is a miracle."

– Albert Einstein

"Take full account of the excellencies which you possess, and in gratitude remember how you would hanker after them, if you had them not."

– Marcus Aurelius

"We often take for granted the very things that most deserve our gratitude."

– Cynthia Ozick

"We can be thankful to a friend for a few acres or a little money; and yet for the freedom and command of the whole earth, and for the great benefits of our being, our life, health, and reason, we look upon ourselves as under no obligation."

– Marcus Annaeus Seneca

"When we become more fully aware that our success is due in large measure to the loyalty, helpfulness, and encouragement we have received from others, our desire grows to pass on similar gifts. Gratitude spurs us on to prove ourselves worthy of what others have done for us. The spirit of gratitude is a powerful energizer."

– Wilfred A. Peterson

"Whatever our individual troubles and challenges may be, it's important to pause every now and then to appreciate all that we have, on every level. We need to literally "count our blessings," give thanks for them, allow ourselves to enjoy them, and relish the experience of prosperity we already have."

— Shakti Gawain

"Thou that has given so much to me,
Give one thing more—a grateful heart;
Not thankful when it pleaseth me,
As if thy blessings had spare days;
But such a heart, whose pulse may be
Thy praise."

— George Herbert

"(Some people) have a wonderful capacity to appreciate again and again, freshly and naively, the basic goods of life, with awe, pleasure, wonder, and even ecstasy."

– A. H. Maslow

"The moment one gives close attention to anything, even a blade of grass, it becomes a mysterious, awesome, indescribably magnificent world in itself."

— Henry Miller

"But the value of gratitude does not consist solely in getting you more blessings in the future. Without gratitude you cannot long keep from dissatisfied thought regarding things as they are."

– Wallace Wattles

"There is a calmness to a life lived in gratitude, a quiet joy."

– Ralph H. Blum

"Gratefulness is the key to a happy life that we hold in our hands, because if we are not grateful, then no matter how much we have we will not be happy — because we will always want to have something else or something more."

— Brother David Steindl-Rast

"Happiness cannot be traveled to, owned, earned, worn or consumed. Happiness is the spiritual experience of living every minute with love, grace and gratitude."

– Denis Waitley

"Real life isn't always going to be perfect or go our way, but the recurring acknowledgement of what is working in our lives can help us not only to survive but surmount our difficulties."

– Sarah Ban Breathnach

"Grace isn't a little prayer you chant before receiving a meal. It's a way to live."

- Attributed to Jacqueline Winspear

"When eating bamboo sprouts, remember the man who planted them."

– Chinese Proverb

"Only a stomach that rarely feels hungry scorns common things."

– Horace

"Blessed are those that can give without remembering and receive without forgetting."

— Unknown

"If you concentrate on finding whatever is good in every situation, you will discover that your life will suddenly be filled with gratitude, a feeling that nurtures the soul."

— Rabbi Harold Kushner

"Nothing that is done for you is a matter of course. Everything originates in a will for the good, which is directed at you. Train yourself never to put off the word or action for the expression of gratitude."

– Albert Schweitzer

"God gave you a gift of 86,400 seconds today. Have you used one to say 'Thank you'?"

- William A. Ward

"Gratitude is a vaccine, an antitoxin, and an antiseptic."

— John Henry Jowett

"The best way to pay for a lovely moment is to enjoy it."

—   Richard Bach

"Both abundance and lack exist simultaneously in our lives, as parallel realities. It is always our conscious choice which secret garden we will tend… when we choose not to focus on what is missing from our lives but are grateful for the abundance that's present — love, health, family, friends, work, the joys of nature and personal pursuits that bring us pleasure — the wasteland of illusion falls away and we experience Heaven on earth."

— Sarah Ban Breathnach

"Whenever we are appreciative, we are filled with a sense of well-being and swept up by the feeling of joy."

– M. J. Ryan

"Gratitude is riches. Complaint is poverty."

— Doris Day

"Many people who order their lives rightly in all other ways are kept in poverty by their lack of gratitude."

– Wallace Wattles

"Let us rise up and be thankful, for if we didn't learn a lot today, at least we learned a little, and if we didn't learn a little, at least we didn't get sick, and if we got sick, at least we didn't die; so, let us all be thankful."

– The Buddha

"Two kinds of gratitude: The sudden kind we feel for what we take; the larger kind we feel for what we give."

- Edwin Arlington Robinson

"Gratitude should not be just a reaction to getting what you want, but an all-the-time gratitude, the kind where you notice the little things and where you constantly look for the good, even in unpleasant situations. Start bringing gratitude to your experiences, instead of waiting for a positive experience in order to feel grateful."

– Marelisa Fábrega

"Gratitude unlocks the fullness of life. It turns what we have into enough, and more. It turns denial into acceptance, chaos to order, confusion to clarity. It can turn a meal into a feast, a house into a home, a stranger into a friend."

– Melody Beattie

"Gratitude is the healthiest of all human emotions. The more you express gratitude for what you have, the more likely you will have even more to express gratitude for."

– Zig Ziglar

"Do not spoil what you have by desiring what you have not; remember that what you now have was once among the things you only hoped for."

– Epicurus

"True forgiveness is when you can say, "Thank you for that experience."

— Oprah Winfrey

"Piglet noticed that even though he had a very small heart, it could hold a rather large amount of gratitude."

– A. A. Milne, Winnie-the Pooh

"True happiness is to enjoy the present, without anxious dependence upon the future, not to amuse ourselves with either hopes or fears but to rest satisfied with what we have, which is sufficient, for he that is so wants nothing. The greatest blessings of mankind are within us and within our reach. A wise man is content with his lot, whatever it may be, without wishing for what he has not."

— Seneca

"Let gratitude be the pillow upon which you kneel to say your nightly prayer. And let faith be the bridge you build to overcome evil and welcome good."

—   Maya Angelou

"If having a soul means being able to feel love and loyalty and gratitude, then animals are better off than a lot of humans."

— James Herriot

"As we express our gratitude, we must never forget that the highest appreciation is not to utter words, but to live by them."

– John F. Kennedy

"My expectations were reduced to zero when I was 21. Everything since then has been a bonus."

— Stephen Hawking

"Gratitude looks to the past and love to the present;
fear, avarice, lust, and ambition look ahead."

—   C. S. Lewis

"When you are grateful, fear disappears and abundance appears."

— Anthony Robbins

"Feeling gratitude and not expressing it is like wrapping a present and not giving it."

– William Arthur Ward

"When we give cheerfully and accept gratefully, everyone is blessed."

– Maya Angelou

"Got no checkbooks, got no banks. Still I'd like to express my thanks - I've got the sun in the mornin' and the moon at night."

— Irving Berlin

"What separates privilege from entitlement is gratitude."

— Brené Brown

"The miracle is not to walk on water. The miracle is to walk on the green earth, dwelling deeply in the present moment and feeling truly alive."

– Thích Nhất Hạnh

"For each new morning with its light,

For rest and shelter of the night,

For health and food, for love and friends,

For everything Thy goodness sends."

— Ralph Waldo Emerson

"When it comes to life the critical thing is whether you take things for granted or take them with gratitude."

—   G. K. Chesterton

"It has been said that life has treated me harshly; and sometimes I have complained in my heart because many pleasures of human experience have been withheld from me…if much has been denied me, much, very much, has been given me…"

— Helen Keller

"Reflect upon your present blessings, of which every man has plenty; not on your past misfortunes, of which all men have some."

– Charles Dickens

"Acknowledging the good that you already have in your life is the foundation for all abundance."

– Eckhart Tolle

"The essence of all beautiful art, all great art, is gratitude."

— Friedrich Nietzsche

"It is not happiness that makes us grateful, but gratefulness that makes us happy."

— Gratefulness.org

"To be grateful is to recognize the love of God in everything."

– Thomas Merton

"Prayer is sitting in the silence until it silences us, choosing gratitude until we are grateful, and praising God until we ourselves are an act of praise."

— Richard Rohr

"You have no cause for anything but gratitude and joy."

—   The Buddha

"Gratitude bestows reverence, allowing us to encounter everyday epiphanies, those transcendent moments of awe that change forever how we experience life and the world."

– John Milton

"There is a law of gratitude, and it is . . . the natural principle that action and reaction are always equal and in opposite directions. The grateful outreaching of your mind in thankful praise to supreme intelligence is a liberation or expenditure of force. It cannot fail to reach that to which it is addressed, and the reaction is an instantaneous movement toward you."

— Wally Wattles

"Be grateful, not only for others, but for yourself."

— Unknown

"Breathe. Let go. And remind yourself that this very moment is the only one you know you have for sure."

– Oprah Winfrey

"Happiness is the realization of God in the heart. Happiness is the result of praise and thanksgiving, of faith, of acceptance; a quiet tranquil realization of the love of God."

— White Eagle

"Live your life so that the fear of death can never enter your heart. When you arise in the morning, give thanks for the morning light. Give thanks for your life and strength. Give thanks for your food and for the joy of living. And if perchance you see no reason for giving thanks, rest assured the fault is in yourself."

– Tecumseh Shawnee Chief

"There is always, always, always something to be thankful for."

– Unknown

"A grateful mind is a great mind which eventually attracts to itself great things."

— Plato

"Be grateful for what you have."

—   Unknown

"Dead people receive more flowers than the living one's because regret is stronger than gratitude."

— Anne Frank

"Everything can be taken from a man but one thing, the last of the human freedoms. To choose one's attitude in any given set of circumstances, to choose one's own way."

– Viktor Frankl

"God has two dwellings; one in heaven, and the other in a meek and thankful heart."

– Izaak Walton

"Showing gratitude is one of the simplest yet most powerful things humans can do for each other."

—   Randy Pausch

"Give thanks for a little and you will find a lot."

— The Hausa of Nigeria

"The miracle of gratitude is that it shifts your perception to such an extent that it changes the world you see."

— Dr. Robert Holden

"He is a wise man who does not grieve for the things which he has not, but rejoices for those which he has."

– Epictetus

"I woke up this morning with devout thanksgiving for my friends, the old and the new."

– Ralph Waldo Emerson

"No one is as capable of gratitude as one who has emerged from the kingdom of the night."

– Elie Wiesel

"No one who achieves success does so without the help of others. The wise and the confident acknowledge this help with gratitude."

- Alfred North Whitehead

"Gratitude is the ability to experience life as a gift. It liberates us from the prison of self-preoccupation."

- John Ortberg

"The deepest craving of human nature is the need to be appreciated."

– William James

"Do not indulge in dreams of having what you have not, but reckon up the chief of the blessings you do possess, and then thankfully remember how you would crave for them if they were not yours."

– Marcus Aurelius

"I would maintain that thanks are the highest form of thought; and that gratitude is happiness doubled by wonder."

— G. K. Chesterton

"If you count all your assets, you always show a profit."

– Robert Quillen

"Gratitude is a quality similar to electricity. It must be produced and discharged and used up in order to exist at all."

—   William Faulkner

"If you want to turn your life around, try thankfulness. It will change your life mightily."

– Gerald Good

"I feel a very unusual sensation – if not indigestion, I think it must be gratitude."

– Benjamin Disraeli

"In the end, though, maybe we must all give up trying to pay back the people in this world who sustain our lives. In the end, maybe it's wiser to surrender before the miraculous scope of human generosity and to just keep saying thank you, forever and sincerely, for as long as we have voices."

— Elizabeth Gilbert

"There is not a more pleasing exercise of the mind than gratitude. It is accompanied with such an inward satisfaction that the duty is sufficiently rewarded by the performance."

— Joseph Addison

"Wake at dawn with a winged heart and give thanks for another day of loving."

— Kahlil Gibran

"Silent gratitude isn't very much to anyone."

– Gertrude Stein

"When you arise in the morning, think of what a precious privilege it is to be alive – to breathe, to think, to enjoy, to love – then make that day count!"

– Steve Maraboli

"Sometimes we should express our gratitude for the small and simple things like the scent of rain, the taste of your favorite food, or the sound of a loved one's voice."

– Joseph B. Wirthlin

"I have walked this earth for 30 years, and, out of gratitude, want to leave some souvenir."

– Vincent van Gogh

"The more you use it, the stronger it grows, and the more power you have to use it on your behalf. If you do not practice gratefulness, its benefaction will go unnoticed, and your capacity to draw on its gifts will be diminished. To be grateful is to find blessings in everything. This is the most powerful attitude to adopt, for there are blessings in everything."

– Alan Cohen

"The root of joy is gratefulness... For it is not joy that makes us grateful; it is gratitude that makes us joyful."

— Brother David Steindl-Rast

"Gratitude goes beyond the 'mine' and 'thine' and claims the truth that all of life is a pure gift. In the past I always thought of gratitude as a spontaneous response to the awareness of gifts received, but now I realize that gratitude can also be lived as a discipline. The discipline of gratitude is the explicit effort to acknowledge that all I am and have is given to me as a gift of love, a gift to be celebrated with joy."

– Henri J.M. Nouwen

"Gratitude causes us to no longer desire a different life. Instead, it causes us to make the most of the one life we already have."

— Joshua Becker

"Gratitude is where self-love begins!"

— Bryant McGill

Thank you to Anna, Ellie, and Sarah for making this project fun and for your invaluable input.

Thank you Google and Jane Friedman for making a daunting task manageable.

Thank you to all who lit the path of gratitude for me. You are the light of the world! Thank you Al, Amanda, Arla, Arnie, Barb, Beka, Bert, Betty, Carrie, Charlie, David, Dave, Dean, Deb, Deidra, Ellen, Gail, Gina, God, Hope, Jana, Jane, Jean, Jessica, Jill, Jim, Jo, Jo Ann, John, Keegan, Kevin, Keylee, Kurt, Larry, Les, Liz, Marnie, Matt[3], Men of Integrity, Men of the Jamaican Mission Trip, Michelle, Mike, Nancy[2], Nick, Patrick, Paul, Peter, Phyllis, Sarah, Sawyer, Scott[2], Shakuntala, Shelly, Steve, Terry[2], Tim, Todd, Tom[2], Tony, Vickie, Wade, and many others!

Made in the USA
Monee, IL
04 May 2026